CBX
SAN JOSE PUBLIC LIBRARY [4]

★ ★ ★

LOS ANGELES
Dodgers

JAMES R. ROTHAUS

CREATIVE EDUCATION

SAN JOSE PUBLIC LIBRARY

Library of Congress Cataloging-in-Publication Data

Rothaus, James.
   Los Angeles Dodgers.

   Summary: A history of the popular baseball team,
covering the years they played in Brooklyn but
emphasizing their activities after they moved to
Los Angeles in 1957.
   1. Los Angeles Dodgers (Baseball team) — History —
Juvenile literature.   [1. Los Angeles Dodgers (Baseball
team) — History.   2. Baseball — History]   I. Title.
GV875.L6R68   1987   796.357'64'0979494   87-22224
ISBN 0-88682-139-8

★ ★ ★
CONTENTS

COVER PHOTO
In 1986, Steve Sax batted .332 with 210 hits and 40 stolen bases—just two points shy of the N.L. batting title.

PHOTO SPREAD (PAGE 2/3)
Rick Monday and Ken Landreaux lead the parade to the clubhouse after the Dodgers put another win in the record books.

The Los Angeles Dodgers stadium has been called the "palace of all baseball parks." It's artfully groomed, ruggedly handsome, and it offers seating for 56,000. Avid fans regularly flock here from all over Southern California to root for their beloved Dodgers. In 1979, Los Angeles became the first team to ever draw more than five million fans to the park in one season.

Yes, the Dodgers have always drawn enthusiastic home crowds, but not just in Los Angeles. The noisy, bustling town of Brooklyn, New York on the other side of the nation was the birthplace of the Dodgers way back in 1897. Let's return now, to those early years, and take a quick look at Dodger baseball in the horse-and-buggy era.

The Dodgers At The Turn Of The Century

In their first National League season, the Dodgers captured the championship. Unfortunately, the history of the Brooklyn team from then on resembles the crazy network of New York streetcars. The nickname "Trolley Dodgers" originally applied to Brooklyn's famous horse-drawn trolley cars, was shortened and applied to the town's baseball team.

For the first 15 years of the century, the Brooklyn Dodgers finished in every spot except first place. The Club's owner, "Squire" Charley Ebbets, and his administration were mostly to blame.

An ambitious man who started with the Dodgers as a peanut hawker, Ebbets went through four managers before settling with Wilbert Robinson who remained at the helm for 18 years. Ebbets himself spent an earlier season managing the team, sending signals from

1901
Led by skipper Ned Nanlon, the original Brooklyn Dodgers finish with 79 victories—good for third place in their very first season in the National League.

PHOTO
The one-and-only Babe Ruth was hired back into big-time baseball as a coach for the 1938 Dodgers.

7

April, 1913
The Dodgers fling
open the doors
to Ebbets field,
their sparkling new
ball park.

the dugout, properly attired in a fashionable black hat.

Ebetts, the smart businessman, quickly realized that Brooklyn was the hottest baseball town in America. The baseball-crazed Brooklynites would almost split the seams of tiny Washington Park during the fierce crosstown rivalry between the Giants and Dodgers. So Ebetts built a much bigger stadium and named it after himself. Ebbets Field, a grand ball park, opened with streaming banners and bright bunting in April, 1913.

Settled in their comfortable stadium, the Dodgers were led into the 1916 World Series by the plump, good-natured Robinson. Brooklyn used the 25 victories of pitcher Jeff Pfiefer, the hefty bats of Zack Wheat and Jake Daubert and a steady defense to earn the right to face the defending World Champion Boston Red Sox.

But the Dodgers hadn't seen anything in the National League like Boston's Babe Ruth, a hard throwing 21-year-old lefty who also toted a mighty bat. Brooklyn lost the Series in five games. The Dodgers spent a long winter waiting for revenge, but they never met Babe Ruth in post-season action again.

Four years later, the Dodgers rode to the 1920 World Series on the arms of seven reliable hurlers, especially Dodger star Burleigh Grimes, "the last legitimate spit-ball pitcher."

In the World Series against the Cleveland Indians, however, the Dodger pitchers stuttered and the Indians waltzed to victory, five games to two.

If those 1920 Dodgers had only known there would be a 21-year drought before their next World Series appearances, perhaps they'd have tried harder.

PHOTO
More than 36,000
fans jammed into
Ebbets Field for the
start of the 1955
Yankees/Dodgers
World Series.

Those Daffy Dodgers Of The 1920's and 30's

During those two fruitless decades, the Brooklyn Dodgers played uneven baseball, finishing no better than fifth 14 times. The caliber of play may not have been all-star quality, but the colorful characters kept the events at Ebbets Field entertaining.

Pitching star Dazzy Vance, the 1924 Most Valuable Player, led the league in ERA three times and in shut-outs four times. When he was off the field or in the clubhouse, however, Vance caused some mischief. He and his practical joker teammates stuck together in the losing years with the motto, "One for all, and oh for four."

Perhaps the daffiest Brooklyn star of that era was Babe Herman. Robinson desperately needed Herman's big bat in the lineup so he tried to overlook Herman's lack of fielding skills—and spent many innings either praying for (or yelling at) his slugger.

Babe had a knack for messing up basic plays, easy pop flies or simple base running. Daydreaming, Herman twice cost the Dodgers runs by loitering on his way around the bases.

Herman once hit a hard liner off the wall with the bases loaded. At the crack of Herman's wicked bat, the runners roared off, churning dirt and confusion. When the dust settled, Chick Fewster was standing on third, Vance was sliding into the same bag from the side facing home and Herman from second. The third baseman was busy tagging each of them with the ball, and the umpire was motioning for a double play!

1916
The Dodgers win the right to play the mighty Boston Red Sox and their superstar Babe Ruth in Brooklyn's first World Series.

PHOTO
Dazzy Vance, Brooklyn's legendary righthander and practical joker, warms up for the 1929 opener at Ebbets Field.

1920
Spitball artist
Burleigh Grimes
leads Dodgers to the
World Series against
the Cleveland
Indians.

Durocher Leads Dodgers To Forties Glory

In 1939, legendary Leo Durocher was hired as player/manager to replace Burleigh Grimes who had proved a much better pitcher than field general. Durocher guided the Dodgers to third place that year, a second in 1940 and into the Series in 1941.

Despite an emotional season of beanballs and rhubarbs, the Dodgers entered the '41 World Series with a strong, unified team, including pitchers Whitlow Wyatt and Kirby Higbe; infielders Dolph Camilli, Pee Wee Reese, Cookie Lavegetto; and outfielders Pete Reiser, Dixie Walker and Joe Medwick.

The Dodgers faced the awesome Yankees, who won five pennants in the 30's. The teams split the first two games, and the Dodgers returned to Ebbets Field. But they left their luck on the other side of the city. The Dodgers lost the first in a series of five championship meetings with the Yankees, four games to one.

As the veteran Dodgers began returning from the battlefields of the Second World War, owner Branch Rickey vowed he was finished with fielding patchwork teams with 16-year-old shortstops and grandfatherly outfielders. He wanted the 1947 pennant, and he took bold steps to get it. He and a young black star, Jackie Robinson, crossed the major league color barrier.

That year, Robinson plugged the Dodgers' hole at first base and was easily named Rookie of the Year. He also blazed the trail for other fine black athletes in the major leagues. He did all this, and first base wasn't even his bag. For most of the years he played for the Dodgers, he was a second-baseman.

PHOTO
The great
Leo Durocher led the
Dodgers into the
1941 Series with
picture-perfect snags
at shortstop.

Two years later, the Dodgers returned to the Series to meet their rivals, the Yankees. With Series veterans Reese, Walker, Reiser, Gil Hodges, Duke Snider and the powerful young battery of Don Newcombe and Roy Campanella, the Dodgers were well armed to take on the Bronx Bombers. Their big guns backfired, however, and the Yankees crushed Brooklyn, four games to one.

The Fabulous Fifties

The 1950's were a whirlwind decade for the Dodgers. Staving off the Giants, they returned to the World Series to face the Yankees in 1952 and 1953 under the direction of skipper Charlie Dressen. But Mickey Mantle and the seemingly unconquerable Yankees proved too much for the National League champs. The Dodgers lost the back-to-back World Series, four games to three, and four to two.

The events preceding the 1953 season shook up the Brooklyn organization. President Branch Rickey had resigned his chair to young Walter O'Malley in 1950. O'Malley was soon disgusted with the repeated trips to the Series only to come home empty-handed. Those seven World Series defeats—five at the hands of the Yankees—were unbearable. Pennants weren't enough for O'Malley, so he replaced Dressen with an unknown manager, Walter Alston, in hopes of changing the Dodgers' fortunes. It was a brilliant strategy.

In his second season as manager, Alston accomplished what no other Dodger skipper had been able to do. He brought a World Championship to Brooklyn.

Those 1955 Dodgers were so explosive that Milwau-

1939
The legendary
Leo Durocher takes
over for the first
of eight seasons
as Dodger manager.

PHOTO
There was a time
when black athletes
were barred from the
major leagues.
Dodger
Jackie Robinson
blazed a new trail
in 1947.

1947
Brooks Robinson
joins the Dodgers
at first base,
becoming the first
black player in the
major leagues, and
picking up Rookie of
the Year honors
in the bargain.

kee's super southpaw, Warren Spahn, wouldn't even face the Brooklyn bats.

Jim Gilliam, Carl Furillo, Campanella, Reese, Snider, and other hard-hitting Dodgers belted their team into the World series against the Yankees that year. Sandy Amoras, a feisty left fielder, completed his first trip to the Series and made an unforgettable crucial catch of a Yogi Berra blast down the left-field line.

Another Dodger, a hard-chucking country boy named Johnny Podres, squelched the Yankees' final threat in the seventh game by retiring Phil Rizzuto, Berra and Hank Bauer. For the first time in history, the Dodgers spent a happy winter celebrating as World Champs. It was to be Brooklyn's last.

The next year they held off the Braves on the last day of the season to clinch the 1956 pennant and the right to defend their crown. Brooklyn was a team steeped in tradition, however, and they fell back into their traditional World Series ways by losing to the Yankees in seven games.

The Dodgers Move To Los Angeles

O'Malley wanted more than a world championship team. He had grand hopes for his Dodgers, but Ebbets Field was a major problem. The splendid old park had been enlarged to hold 32,000, almost twice the number as it originally held, yet it still couldn't seat the hoards of Brooklynites who wanted to watch the Dodgers. It simply could not be remodeled. He searched every block of Brooklyn for a plot of land large enough to hold a bigger stadium, but none was available. So, he began searching for a new home—

PHOTO
The whistling bat
of Harry Lavagetto
brought smiles to his
teammates during
this 1939 batting
practice.

PHOTO ABOVE
Steve Garvey's idol
was Dodger superstar
Gil Hodges, shown
here sliding safely
in 1949 action.

PHOTO AT RIGHT
Dodger manager
Walter Alston brought
a world championship
to New York before
moving with his team
to L.A.

1950
Walter O'Malley
takes over as
President and vows
to bring the
World Championship
to Brooklyn.

a new city — for the Dodgers.

O'Malley looked toward the rapidly developing West, and he saw that his dreams could become reality. He knew almost immediately that Los Angeles was destined to be the new home of the Dodgers.

One team in California wouldn't be enough, he thought, so he convinced the rival Giants to move to San Francisco.

During the winter of '57-58, the Dodgers and Giants moved their players, families and equipment across the nation. The fans in New York were heartbroken; the fans in California were jubilant.

Although L.A. fans eagerly embraced the boys in blue, the Dodgers' first year in southern California wasn't very rosy. Catcher Roy Campanella was paralyzed in a tragic auto accident a few weeks before spring training. Ace pitcher Don Newcombe never won a game in a Los Angeles uniform; he was traded in June. Age was catching up with Dodger heroes Gilliam, Reese, Snider and Furillo.

"It was a drab performance," explains Dodger historian Tommy Holmes, "but Los Angeles was so excited about major league baseball that the fans did not seem to notice. Home attendance that first year was 1,845,556, a gain of more than 800,000 over the final year at Ebbets Field. On August 30, for a game with the Giants, a paying crowd of 78,672 showed up, a bit more than twice as many as could possibly have crammed into Ebbets Field."

Amazingly, the Dodgers recovered from a seventh-place finish in 1958 to capture the 1959 World Series!

Seventeen Dodger victories during the '59 campaign came from an electrifying arm of a young pitcher,

PHOTO
Dodger catcher
Roy Campanella had
a cannon for an arm.
He anchored the
1955 World Champs.

Don Drysdale. Early in the season, unknown shortstop Maury Wills was called up from the minors, and dazzled everyone.

Still, it was a struggle to win the pennant. A tie at the end of the regular season forced a three-game playoff. The Dodgers captured the first game. Gil Hodges trotted home on an error in the twelfth inning to allow the Dodgers to win the second game marathon. The Dodgers went on to the World Series for the tenth time.

The American League champion Chicago White Sox were no match for the Dodger veterans and all their World Series experience. Podres and Drysdale tossed great games, but the real Series pitching hero was right-handed reliever Larry Sherry who was credited with two saves and two victories.

The Astonishing Koufax Era

The years following the 1959 championship can simply be labeled the Koufax era. Sanford Brown Koufax was a hard-throwing bonus baby when he first joined Brooklyn in 1955. He struggled for control during his first few campaigns, but finally began to show flashes of the great Hall-of-Famer he'd soon become. Between 1960 and 1966, the success of the Dodgers rested on the zip and sting of the Koufax fastball, change-up and curve.

In 1962, everyone blamed Koufax's sore finger as the reason the Giants captured the National League pennant from the Dodgers in a best-of-three playoff.

In 1963, Koufax went 25-5 on the mound. As the National League MVP, his 1.88 era was the lowest in 20 years. The Dodgers jetted to the World Series that year

1955
In his second season as Brookyn's skipper, Walter Alston leads the Bronx Bombers to their first and only World Championship.

PHOTO
Don Drysdale mowed down dozens of enemy batters as the Dodgers marched to a 1959 World Series crown.

against New York. Koufax set a series record by striking out 15 Yankees, and the astonishing Dodgers swept the series in four straight.

In 1964, a bad pitch in mid-August sidelined the ace for the rest of the season with a sore left elbow. That injury also sunk L.A.'s hopes for back-to-back titles. They finished a disappointing sixth.

In 1965, Koufax was back, and he was superb. He racked up 382 strikeouts, pitched his fourth no-hitter and took home his second Cy Young Award. His 26 victories, Drysdale's 25 and Claude Osteen's 15 propelled the Dodgers into the 1965 World Series.

L.A. dropped the first two games against the Twins. But back in Dodger Stadium, Osteen, Drysdale and Koufax pitched crucial victories. The teams returned to Minnesota, the Dodgers up by a game. Osteen lost the sixth game, and the Series was tied. Alston had a tough decision: pitch Koufax with only two days rest, or Drysdale with three. He chose Koufax, and he was right. The Dodgers shut out the Twins 2-0.

The Dodgers returned to defend their championship in 1966 against the Baltimore Orioles. Pitching was no problem for Los Angeles. They simply couldn't score. They managed only two runs in the entire Series and were shut out in their final 33 innings. Osteen pitched valiantly in the third game, tossing a three-hitter. Unfortunately, one of those hits was a Paul Blair homer. In the final game, Drysdale threw a four-hitter, but one was a home run by Frank Robinson.

The fate of the 1967 Dodgers was determined before they even began spring training. During the off season, and only a few days after he had received his third

1958
O'Malley moves the Dodgers to Los Angeles; Dodger superstar Roy Campanella is paralyzed in a tragic auto accident.

PHOTO AT LEFT
Smiling Frank Robinson provided some of the few high spots during the early 1970's.

PHOTO SPREAD NEXT PAGE
Smokey the Bear teams up with Dodger infield star Steve Sax during a break in the action at Dodger Stadium. (1986)

1959
Led by
skipper Walter
"Smokey" Alston,
the Los Angeles
Dodgers win their
first World
Championship after
finishing a lowly
seventh the year
before.

Cy Young Award, the mighty Koufax announced his retirement.

"I just can't go through the agony of pitching anymore," he explained sadly. "The pain in my arm is too intense." Doctors feared Koufax's arm might have to be amputated if he continued to pitch.

Koufax retired to his home town of Brooklyn where his remarkable career had begun only eleven years before. He won 129 games and lost 47. In his last four years his record was a phenomenal 97-27. He tossed 40 shutouts during his career, led the league in strikeouts four times, and had the lowest ERA for five straight years. He held the record of four no-hitters until Houston's Nolan Ryan beat that total in 1981.

Building Toward The '81 World Championship

With Koufax's retirement, the Dodgers embarked on an eight-year dry spell. No World Series appearances. Not one.

During those lean years, many top athletes wore Dodger blue, including Willie Davis, Richie Allen, and the great Frank Robinson. Eventually all were traded for hot young pitchers Andy Messersmith, Tommy John and Don Sutton.

The frequent losses didn't depress the optimistic Dodgers who were busily developing future stars in their minor league system. Finally the future arrived.

In 1974, Alston fielded a strong young team. Steve Garvey, 26, was now a fantastic, durable first baseman and the National League Most Valuable Player. Davey Lopes, 29, was handling the second base and lead-off chores with excellence. Bill Russell, 25, had devel-

PHOTO
The "man with the golden arm."
Tommy John helped whisk the Dodgers into the '78 Series against the Yanks.

28

1962
Maury Wills steals
a record 104 bases
in a single season
to shatter Ty Cobb's
old record of 96.

oped into a consistent shortstop. Ron Cey ("The Penguin"), was a standout at third base. He was the forty-fourth player to play the Dodger hotspot since they moved to L.A., and he proved worth the wait.

These infielders, a host of young pitchers, catcher Steve Yeager, and outfielders Joe Ferguson, Bill Buckner and Jimmy Wynn led the team to an exciting World Series battle with the Oakland Athletics. The jittery young Dodgers couldn't quite overcome the nervousness which plagued this first Series appearance, and the A's took the title, four games to one.

In both 1977 and 1978, the Dodgers made it to the World Series against the New York Yankees. Oh, those Yanks! Like the Brooklyn teams of yesteryear, L.A. crumbled under the Bronx Bombers in both series.

Since 1974, the Dodgers had strived valiantly to regain the world title. Each year they had come close, winning the N.L. West division four times. Finally, in 1981 they won it all — but, not without a struggle.

Stalwarts Cey, Russell, Lopes and Garvey began the year as the major league's longest-lasting group of infielders. They were joined by veteran fielders Dusty Baker, Rick Monday and Reggie Smith, along with experienced pitchers "Happy" Hooton, Terry Forester and a crop of exciting young hurlers.

The year started with a bang. The entire nation caught Fernandomania. Fernando Valenzuela, a screwball pitcher from Mexico, was a 20-year-old who barely spoke English, but his baseball lingo was perfectly clear. He roared off to an 8-0 start. He was the force behind the Division-leading Dodgers when suddenly all baseball stopped because of a league-wide players' strike.

PHOTO
Tommy Lasorda,
the "True-Blue"
Dodger Manager, is
shown having one of
his friendly chats
with a N.L. umpire.

When play resumed after the strike, the Dodgers met the Astros for the Division title. The Astros won the first two, but the Dodgers then won three straight. They then defeated Montreal for the National League pennant, earning the right to meet the Yankees in the World Series.

Fierce Yankee reliever Goose Gossage, who reminded many L.A. fans of Don Drysdale, used his fastball to save the first two games for the Yanks. At that point, most people figured the Dodgers would lose to New York *again*. But Fernando and his teammates went to work on their home turf. Valenzuela locked up the N.L. Rookie of the Year and Cy Young Awards with his gutsy 5-4 victory in the third game. It was the first of four straight Dodger victories. The Yankee hex had been broken at last, and the Dodgers were World Champs!

Never before had three players shared the Most Valuable Player award. Dodgers Ron Cey, Steve Yeager and Pedro Guerrero split the honors. It was the best possible tribute to Dodger teamwork.

Changing Faces Of The 80's

Beginning in 1982, the Dodgers began a rebuilding program that would continue for several seasons.

It is always sad to see old, familiar faces disappear from a close-knit "family" like the Dodgers.

It is difficult, too, for the young guys who come in to replace the popular veterans.

Suppose, for example, that your name is Steve Sax. You're a raw rookie, and you wonder deep-down if you really have what it takes to play in the majors. Suddenly,

1963
N.L. MVP
Sandy Koufax sets a new World Series strikeout record by mowing down 15 Yankees, as the Dodgers sweep the Yanks in four straight.

PHOTO
Bushy-haired Don Sutton in electrifying Dodger performance of the early 1980's.

1965
Dodger pitchers Koufax, Drysdale and Osteen team up for 66 victories to propel the Dodgers to another World Championship.

PHOTO
The legendary Sandy Koufax struck out 18 batters in a single game on two different occasions— Aug. 31, 1954, and Apr. 24, 1962.

the phone rings. A deep, male voice tells you matter-of-factly that you've been tabbed to replace the ever-popular Davey Lopes at second. What thoughts run through your mind?

"Well, you're sure excited" said Sax, when asked a question by a reporter from *Sporting News.* "In the back of your mind, though, you have this funny feeling, like, 'Hey, 50,000 people are going to be up in the stands watching every move, wondering why this kid is standing on second where Davey is supposed to be.' You definitely feel those eyes looking down."

Actually, a total of 3.6 million pairs of eyes (an all-time major league record) watched Sax, the unknown rookie, become Sax the National League Rookie of the Year over the course of the 1982 campaign. Along the way, he batted .282, set a club record for stolen bases by a rookie (49), and played superbly and confidently in the infield.

Believe it or not, Sax was the fourth straight Dodger to be named N.L. Rookie of the Year.

"Hey, I'm proud of the award," shrugged Steve, "but the most important thing about this season for me was getting to play with some of the guys I've admired for so long—*before* they left the club."

Steve was referring, of course, to guys like Steve Garvey and Ron Cey, members of the famous Dodger infield unit that had begun playing together when Sax was still in junior high. At season's end, Garvey signed on with the Padres, and Cey was traded to the Cubs. With those major moves, the Dodger rebuilding program was thrown into high gear.

Most teams are expected to "bite the bullet" during a rebuilding year.

"Yeah, I've heard it said that you shouldn't expect to contend for a year or two until the new guys get used to each other," said Dodger Manager Lasorda at the midway point of the '83 season.

"But, what kind of talk is that?" continued Tommy. "That's not Dodger talk, at least I never hear that stuff 'round here. You tell guys like Steve Sax, Mike Marshall, Greg Brock or Fernando that they got no business winning a pennant, and they'll look at you like you've lost your marbles."

Sure enough, the Dodgers eventually edged out Ted Turner's Atlanta Braves to become champs of the Western Division that year. Led by veteran Pedro Guerrero (32 homers and 103 RBIs), the youngsters really took it to the rest of the division. Greg Brock smashed 20 home runs; Mike Marshall batted .292; Steve Sax made only six errors in the entire second half; and Valenzuela threw for 15 victories.

Even though Lasorda's "kids" were finally mowed down by the Phillies in the N.L. Championship Series, three games to one, the Dodger manager came away with a good feeling about the season.

"Hey, lots of people figured us for patsies at the start of the year," he said with his best I-told-you-so look. "What can I say? They're good, and they'll get better."

Not so fast, Tommy. The very next season—1984— those same Dodgers toppled to fourth with a record of 79-83. It was only the second time in 16 years that the club lost more games than it won.

Dodger Vice President Al Campanis blamed the skid on injuries.

"People falling down—that's what I'll remember about this season," he grumbled, pointing to a row of 15

1974
Young Steve Garvey wins N.L. MVP award.

PHOTO
Courageous
Ron "The Penguin" Cey was beaned by a pitch in the 1981 World Series, but was back in the batting cage for the next game.

PHOTO ABOVE
Lightning-quick
Maury Wills was
swift at shortstop, but
even swifter on the
basepaths as the
Dodgers top thief in
the early 60's.

PHOTO AT RIGHT
First baseman
Steve Garvey
sparked the famous
Dodger infield that
terrorized the
National League in
the 1970's and
early 1980's.

Dodgers who had spent time on the disabled list.

Lasorda had a different theory. He figured the club's decision to cut veteran outfielder Dusty Baker before the season may have put a bigger load on Pedro Guerrero, the last remaining old-timer.

"Pedro was really pressing at the beginning of the season," said Tommy. "I think he was trying to carry the club, but it backfired on him. Instead he slumped a bit, and that probably cost us a few games.

"No sweat, though," said the ever-optimistic manager as he tucked his thumbs below his ample belly. "Nice thing about baseball is you've always got next year."

One More Time!

Sports reporters for the Los Angeles papers spent a good portion of the 1985 season thinking up new ways to describe Mariano Duncan. He was the new Dodger shortstop, a kid called up from the Dodger farm system for a "look-see" early in the season. But he was more than that.

"He is the Flying Burrito Brothers, all jammed into Dodger Blue," wrote one reporter after witnessing Mariano in action for the first time.

"A kangaroo in cleats," wrote another.

"Baseball's answer to the guy in the cape who leaps tall buildings," wrote another.

"A spring-loaded human — at least, I *think* he's human," wrote yet another.

In the *Official Baseball Guide,* Gordon Verrell summed up Mariano's contribution in concrete terms:

"What Duncan, the most exciting infielder the Dodgers have brought along in years, did was solidify a de-

1977
In his first
full season as
Dodger skipper,
Tommy Lasorda leads
Dodgers to the World
Series. He repeats
the feat in '78.

PHOTO
Dodger left fielder
Dusty Baker flies into
second against the
Mets at Shea
Stadium.

fense that was all thumbs the first two months of the season when the club was charged with 62 errors. The Dodgers still wound up leading the league in errors with 166, and 30 of those were committed by Duncan, but the rookie was able to make many outstanding plays on hits that would have gone through the Dodger infield of years past."

Sparked in part by Duncan, the Dodgers ignited for their fifth Division Championship in nine years. Give credit to . . . well, everyone.

Start with Pedro Guerrero who clobbered 15 homers just during the month of June!

For an encore, Pedro went out and batted .460 in July. He wasn't alone, though. Greg Brock, Ken Landreaux and Mike Marshall combined for 61 homers in '85. Mariano Duncan pilfered a team-high 38 bases. Fernando was fantastic, pitching 17 victories, including five shutouts, but he was still outclassed by Oral Hershiser. The rookie phenom went 19-3 with five shutouts!

Oh yes, and don't forget the guys who slammed the door. Tom Niedenfuer and Ken Howell came in from the bullpen for 31 deeply-appreciated saves that year.

For the sixth time in eight seasons, over 3 million spectators poured through the turnstiles at Dodger Stadium. "Champs again!" roared the Dodger fans.

Then a giant shadow swept across the city, as the mighty St. Louis Cardinals flew into town for the National League Championship Series. When L.A. took the first two games, the baby-faced Dodgers were thinking "World Series."

But it was not to be. In the end, it was the older, more experienced Cardinals who finally triumphed in six.

1981
Rookie pitcher Fernando Valenzuela wins N.L. Rookie of the Year and Cy Young awards while leading the Dodgers to a World Series victory over the New York Yankees. Cey, Yeager and Guerrero are the first trio in history to share Series MVP honors.

PHOTO
Dodger catcher Steve Yeager closes the door.

1982
Steve Sax wins N.L.
Rookie of the Year
honors; Steve Garvey
and Ron Cey play
their final seasons
in Dodger Blue.

The Dodgers fell from their perch atop the division in 1986, but Fernando Valenzuela soared.

"Fernando did more than merely dominate," gushed a writer for *Bill Mazeroski's Baseball* chronicle.

"He composed symphonies. He was Van Gogh at the canvas. He raised pitching to a level beyond balls and strikes and ERAs. He had no bullpen, and no offense. He had no defense. All he had were five spectacular pitches and the natural-born know-how up there in his noggin. And he used them to rise above the mediocrity around him and become the first Dodger to win 20 since Tommy John in 1977."

Dodger fans will remember Fernando, but they will try to forget the season.

On April 3, 1986, superstar Pedro Guerrero wiped out his knee while sliding in an exhibition game. From there, the year went haywire for Los Angeles.

The '86 Dodgers committed more errors in a single season than any other major league team in the previous five years. They lost their most games (89) since 1967. They had their worst road record since 1905, and they came just one-half game away from becoming the first National League team in history to go from first to last in one season.

Somehow, though, Tommy Lasorda found a way to put the whole catastrophe in a nicer light. "We proved that even the best baseball organizations can have a bad year, that's all," and then he looked up and winked. "We won the division title in 1981, '83 and '85, right? Well, 1987 is an odd-numbered year, too."

PHOTO
Bill Russell,
Davey Lopes,
Ron Cey and
Steve Garvey were
an awesome infield.
Here, Russell stops
an Atlanta thief
in 1981 action.

1986
Fernando Valenzuela
becomes the first
Dodger pitcher since
Tommy John in 1977
to win 20 games
in a single season.

Pedro Guerrero was back, hale and hearty. A quick look down the opening day roster showed that Sax, Duncan, Madlock, Marshall, Stubbs, Landreaux, Scioscia, Valenzuela, Hershiser, Welch, Howell and Honeycutt were all back, too.

For the most part, these were the very same Dodgers who had steamrolled the entire division back in 1985, only better. You see, thanks to the whipping they took in 1986, these guys were leaner, hungrier and far more experienced than ever before.

Behind them, waiting anxiously in the wings, were the talented young men in the fabulous Los Angeles farm system who were itching to take their turn in Dodger Blue. Now. Or next year. Or, in those long, lazy baseball summers of the 1990's and beyond.

PHOTO
The "Great Fernando!"
Dodger ace Fernando Valenzuela completed 20 of his 34 starts, winning 21 games and compiling a 3.14 ERA during the 1986 campaign.